Facts About the Arabian Oryx

By Lisa Strattin

© 2016 Lisa Strattin

Revised © 2022 Lisa Strattin

FREE BOOK

FREE FOR ALL SUBSCRIBERS

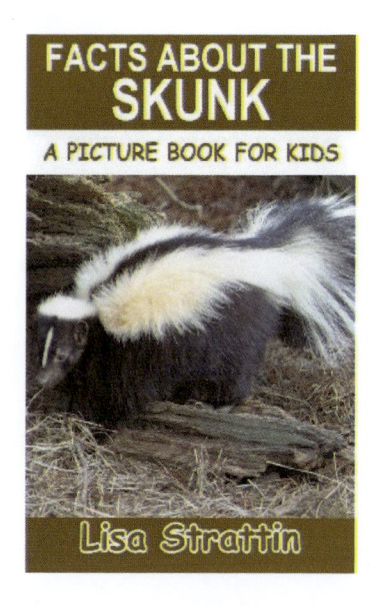

FACTS ABOUT THE SKUNK

A PICTURE BOOK FOR KIDS

Lisa Strattin

LisaStrattin.com/Subscribe-Here

BOX SET

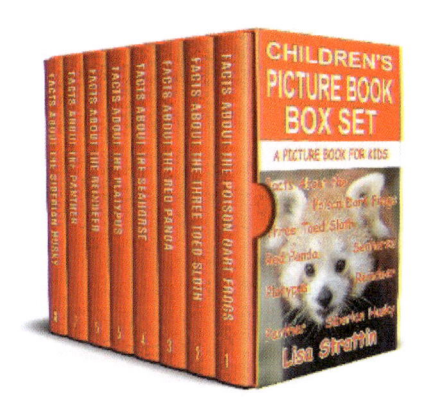

- **FACTS ABOUT THE POISON DART FROGS**
- **FACTS ABOUT THE THREE TOED SLOTH**
  - **FACTS ABOUT THE RED PANDA**
  - **FACTS ABOUT THE SEAHORSE**
  - **FACTS ABOUT THE PLATYPUS**
  - **FACTS ABOUT THE REINDEER**
  - **FACTS ABOUT THE PANTHER**
- **FACTS ABOUT THE SIBERIAN HUSKY**

LisaStrattin.com/BookBundle

Facts for Kids Picture Books by Lisa Strattin

Little Blue Penguin, Vol 92

Chipmunk, Vol 5

Frilled Lizard, Vol 39

Blue and Gold Macaw, Vol 13

Poison Dart Frogs, Vol 50

Blue Tarantula, Vol 115

African Elephants, Vol 8

Amur Leopard, Vol 89

Sabre Tooth Tiger, Vol 167

Baboon, Vol 174

Sign Up for New Release Emails Here

LisaStrattin.com/subscribe-here

All rights reserved. No part of this book may be reproduced by any means whatsoever without the written permission from the author, except brief portions quoted for purpose of review.

All information in this book has been carefully researched and checked for factual accuracy. However, the author and publisher makes no warranty, express or implied, that the information contained herein is appropriate for every individual, situation or purpose and assume no responsibility for errors or omissions. The reader assumes the risk and full responsibility for all actions, and the author will not be held responsible for any loss or damage, whether consequential, incidental, special or otherwise, that may result from the information presented in this book.

All images are free for use or purchased from stock photo sites or royalty free for commercial use.

Some coloring pages might be of the general species due to lack of available images.

I have relied on my own observations as well as many different sources for this book and I have done my best to check facts and give credit where it is due. In the event that any material is used without proper permission, please contact me so that the oversight can be corrected.

★★COVER IMAGE★★

https://www.flickr.com/photos/cuatrok77/9646484043/

★★ADDITIONAL IMAGES★★

https://www.flickr.com/photos/cuatrok77/14971729358/

https://www.flickr.com/photos/cuatrok77/15463468988/

https://www.flickr.com/photos/cuatrok77/13958070025/

https://www.flickr.com/photos/timevanson/7824938022/

https://www.flickr.com/photos/ksblack99/24107087137/

https://www.flickr.com/photos/shankaronline/8454554499/

https://www.flickr.com/photos/93882360@N07/12801282143/

https://www.flickr.com/photos/93882360@N07/12801282143/

https://www.flickr.com/photos/big-ashb/10315334643/

https://www.flickr.com/photos/jaygalvin/48752567028/

Contents

- INTRODUCTION 9
- CHARACTERISTICS 11
- APPEARANCE 13
- LIFE STAGES 15
- LIFE SPAN 17
- SIZE 19
- HABITAT 21
- DIET 23
- FRIENDS AND ENEMIES 25
- SUITABILITY AS PETS 27

INTRODUCTION

The Arabian Oryx looks like a white, overweight deer with straight dark horns. Some of its closest relatives are bison, buffalo, sheep, and domestic cattle. As its name suggests, the Arabian Oryx lives on the Arabian Peninsula, a large area of mostly desert that sits between Africa and Asia.

Fifty years ago, the Arabian Oryx was classified as extinct in the wild. However, after several successful breeding programs in zoos and in private collections, it was reintroduced, into the wild, across its native territory throughout the 1980's and 1990's. In 2011, it became the first animal to have gone from being extinct in the wild to having its status upgraded to 'vulnerable' by the International Union for Conservation of Nature, with a population in the wild of over a thousand animals.

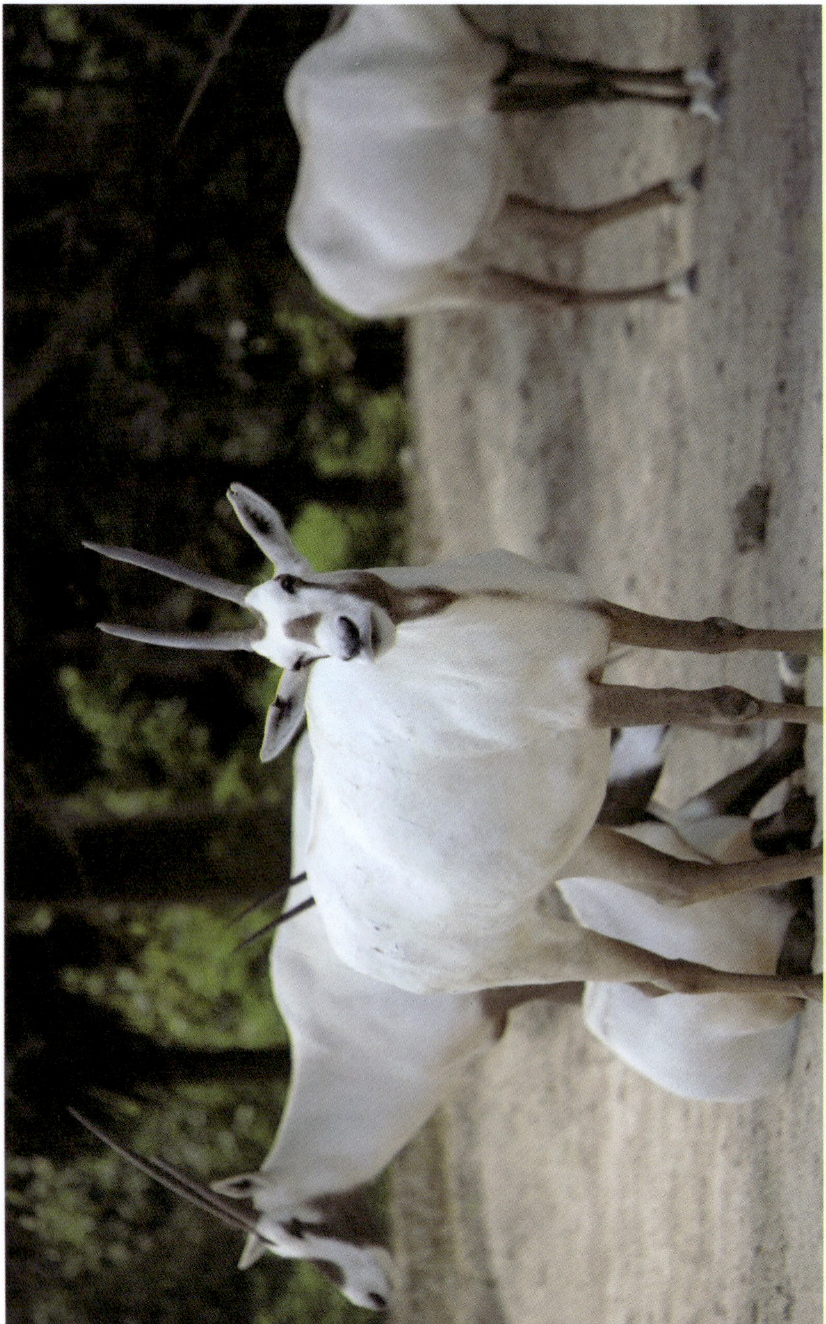

CHARACTERISTICS

Arabian Oryxes have been known to travel in herds of as many as 100 animals, though herds as small as 10 are more common. This may be due to how few wild animals there are because other kinds of Oryxes have been known to travel in herds in excess of 600 animals!

Oryxes have an excellent sense of smell and are able to sense rain from a long distance away. When it smells rain, a herd will travel a great distance to find it, because after a rain in the desert, the green plants that the Oryx eats will grow thicker and more lush. Because of this growth, Arabian Oryxes may range over vast areas, as much as 1,200 square miles, which is bigger than the state of Rhode Island int eh U.S.

Oryxes are very well adapted to their desert homes, and its ability to go without water rivals that of the camel.

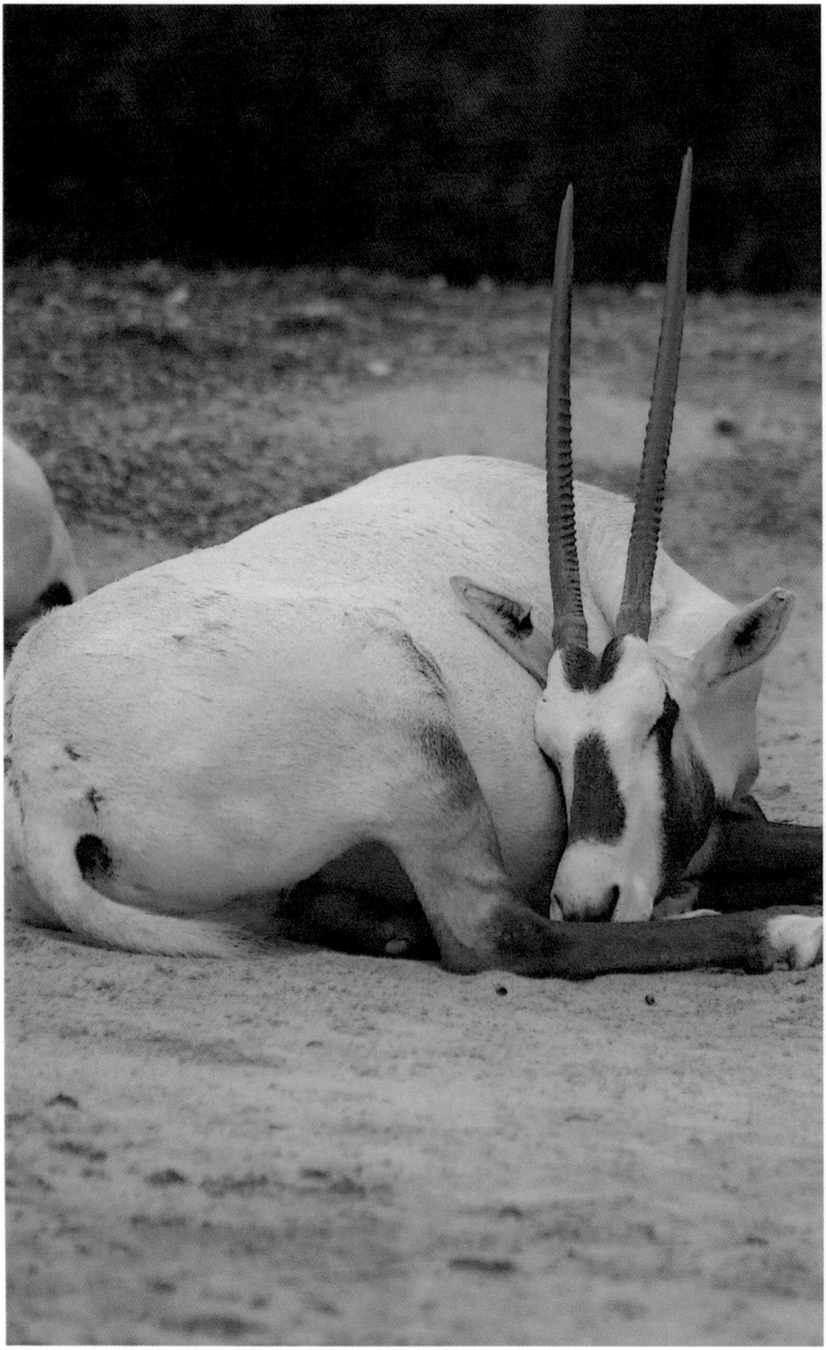

APPEARANCE

Under its white coat, its skin is very dark, which is thought to protect it from the sun's ultra-violet rays. This dark skin protects them from getting sun burned, much in the same way that sunscreen lotion can protect us from getting burned on a summer day.

The Arabian Oryx has long, thin horns that range in color from gray to black, and grow to be as long as five feet, which is nearly as tall as an average man. Some people claim that the horns on these animals are what gave rise to the legend of the unicorn, when seen from its side, the oryx is a majestic, white beast, and its pair of long horns can line up to look like one single horn.

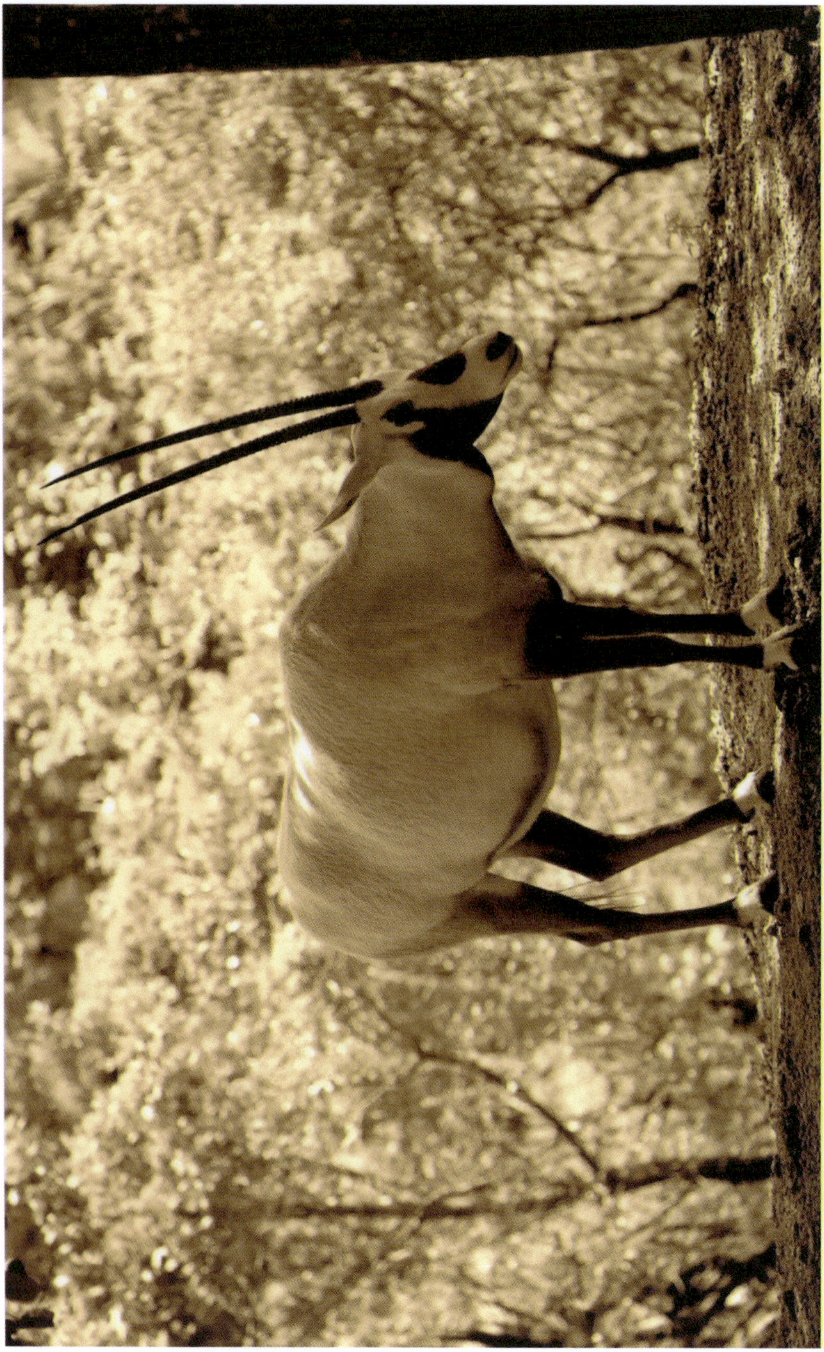

LIFE STAGES

Like most mammals, Arabian Oryxes give birth to live young. Mothers are pregnant for around nine months, and usually leave the herd to give birth in private. Calves are able to walk within minutes of being born but are kept separate from the herd for two to three weeks. During these first weeks of a calf's life, it will be left alone for long periods of time, while its mother spends much of her time with the herd and returns to the calf several times a day to nurse it.

After these first few weeks, when the calf has joined the herd, it will stay with its mother for as long as nine months and will reach maturity in about two years.

As soon as they are old enough, adult males will leave their mother's herd and find another herd with which to live.

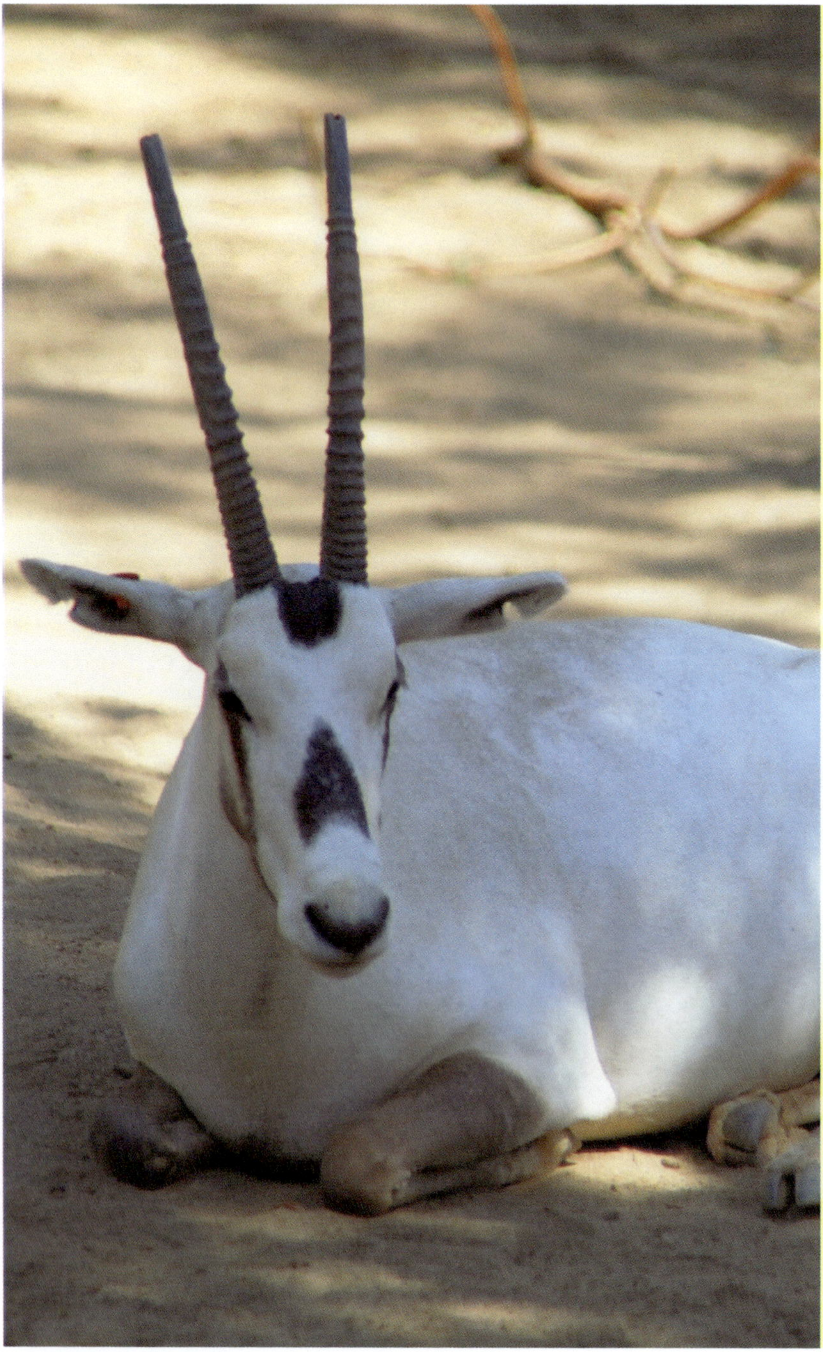

LIFE SPAN

In captivity, Arabian Oryxes have been known to live for twenty years or more. In the wild though, where they face regular droughts, dehydration, and predators, they probably don't live quite as long.

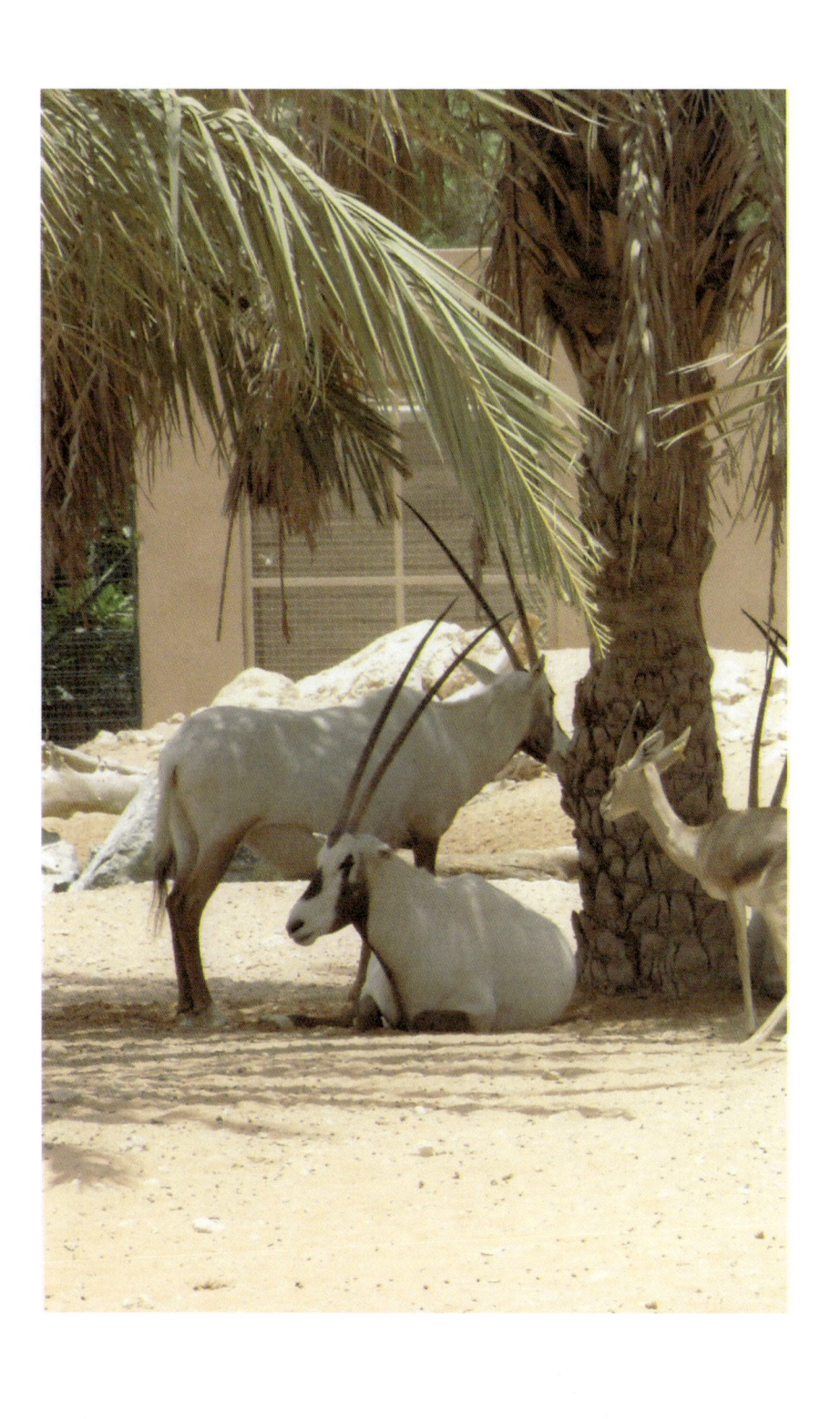

SIZE

An Arabian Oryx stands about 40 inches at the shoulder or is about as tall as some second or third graders. However, at 150 pounds, it can weigh as much as a full grown person.

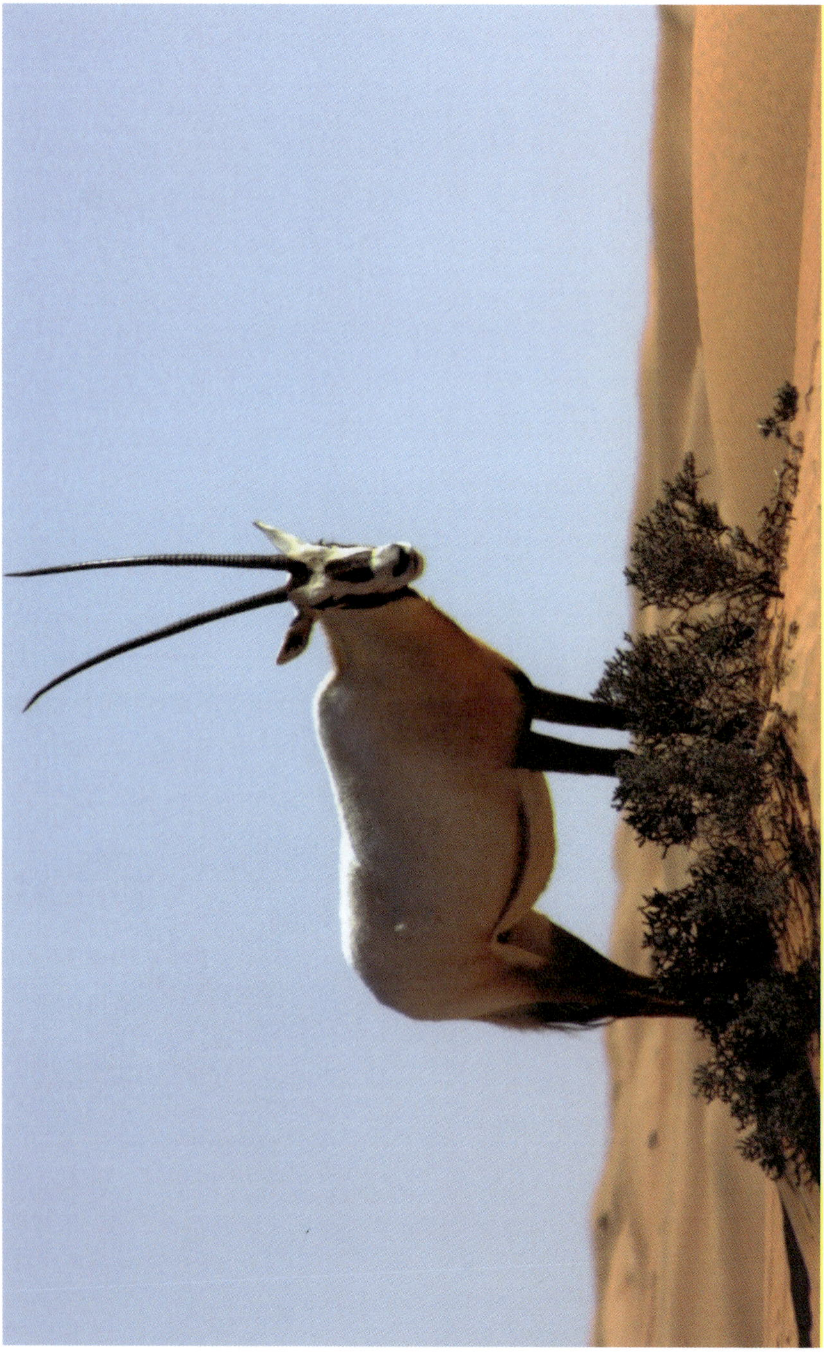

HABITAT

Oryxes are true desert dwellers and, true to their name, Arabian Oryxes inhabit the deserts of the Arabian Peninsula, a large area of land that between Africa and Asia, made up of the countries of the United Arab Emirates, Saudi Arabia, Yemen, and Oman. These animals have been found to roam farther north, as well, into Iraq and Syria.

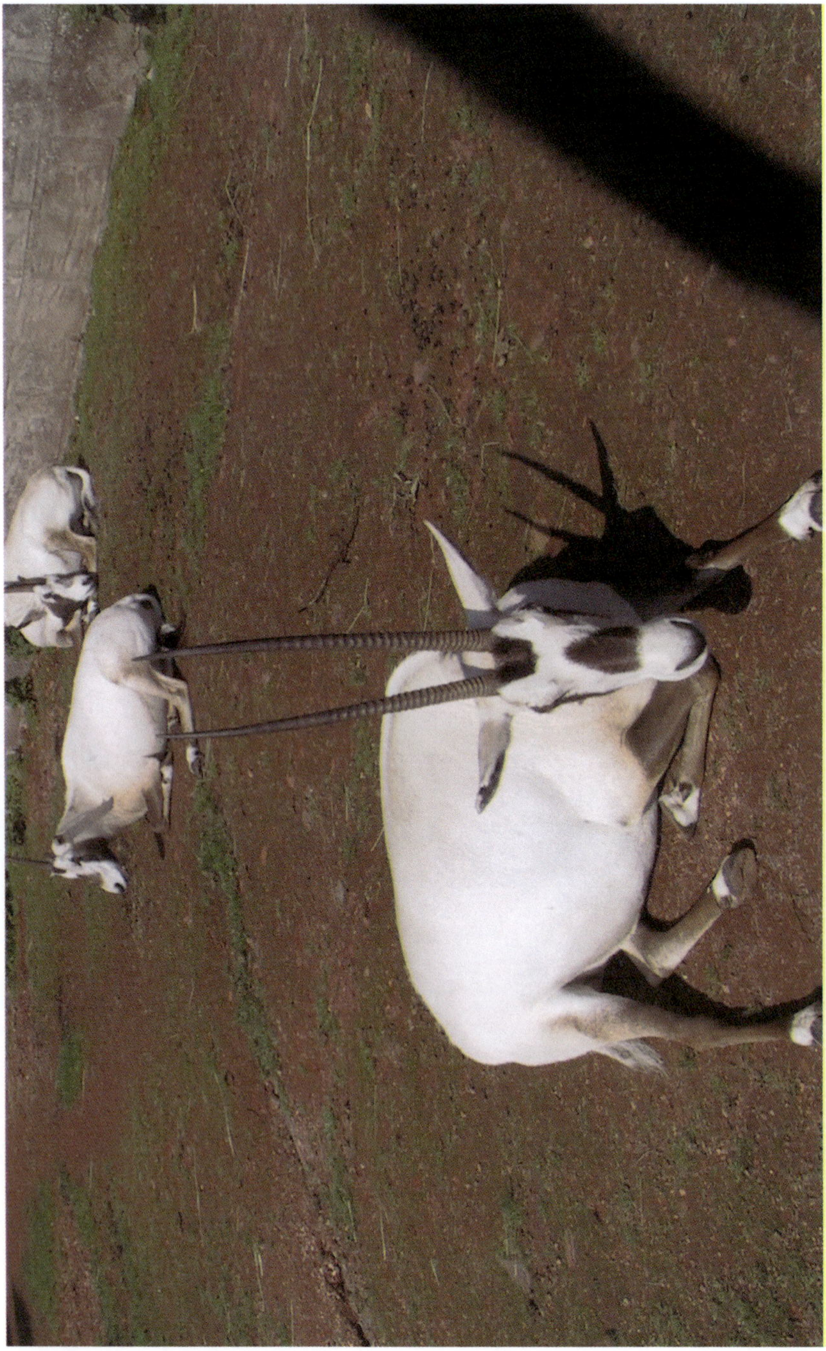

DIET

Oryxes thrive on grasses, though they'll also eat roots, fruits, and the buds of trees when they can find them.

Like many other desert dwellers, they get the water they need from the plants they eat. They do this in part by eating early in the morning, this way they are able to also take in any dew that has collected on the leaves.

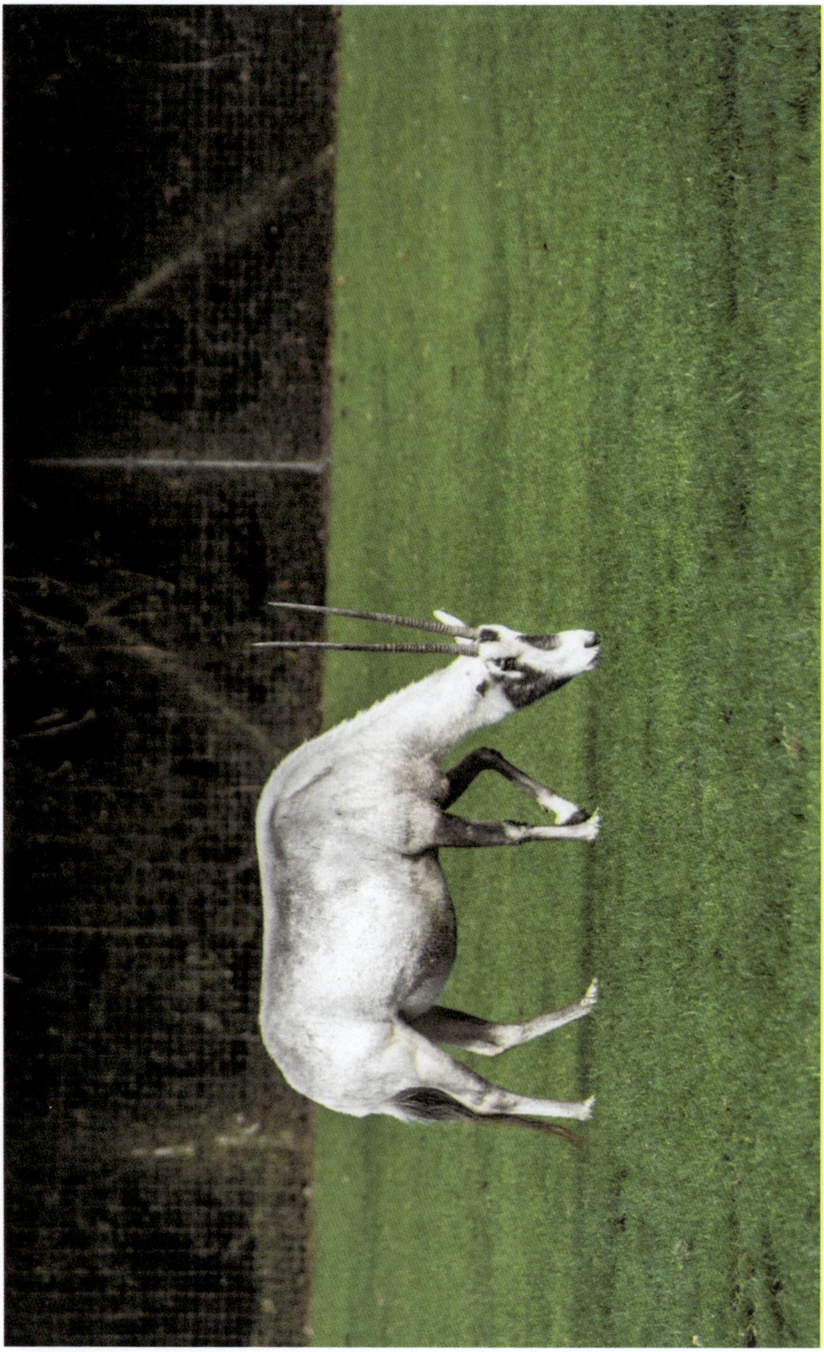

FRIENDS AND ENEMIES

Some of the Arabian Oryx's friendly neighbors would include camels, hyenas, foxes and gazelles.

Wolves are considered to be their only natural predator.

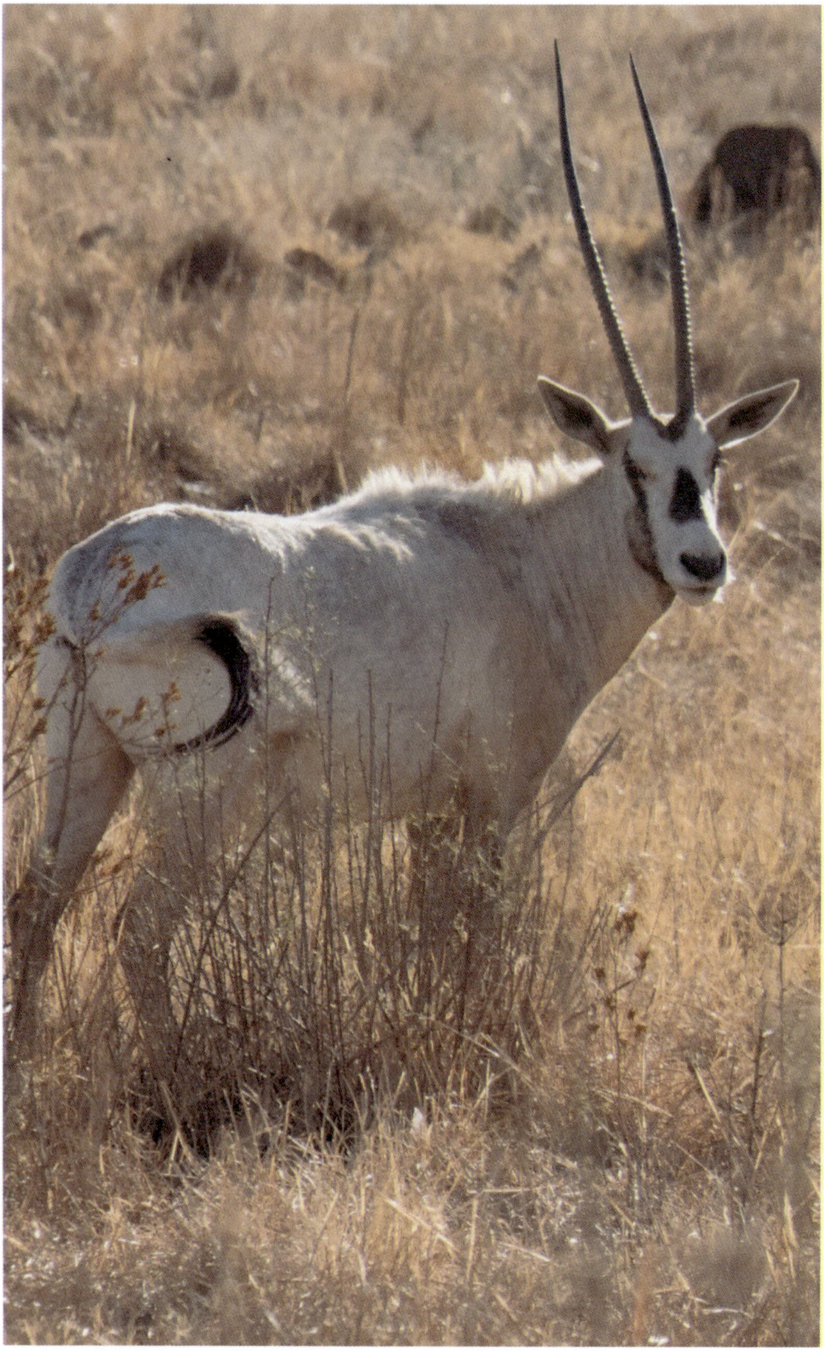

SUITABILITY AS PETS

While the Arabian Oryx has done well in captivity, unlike horses and cows it is not a domesticated animal. If scared, it will use its very long, spear-like horns to defend itself; imagine trying to pet an animal that wanted to stab you with its long horns!

In zoos and in private collections, the Oryx would be allowed to feed on naturally grown grasses or, if in an enclosed pen, fed hay and hay-pellets. It only comes into contact with zoo keepers under very controlled circumstances.

So, as you can imaging, the Arabian Oryx is not suitable to be a pet in your backyard!

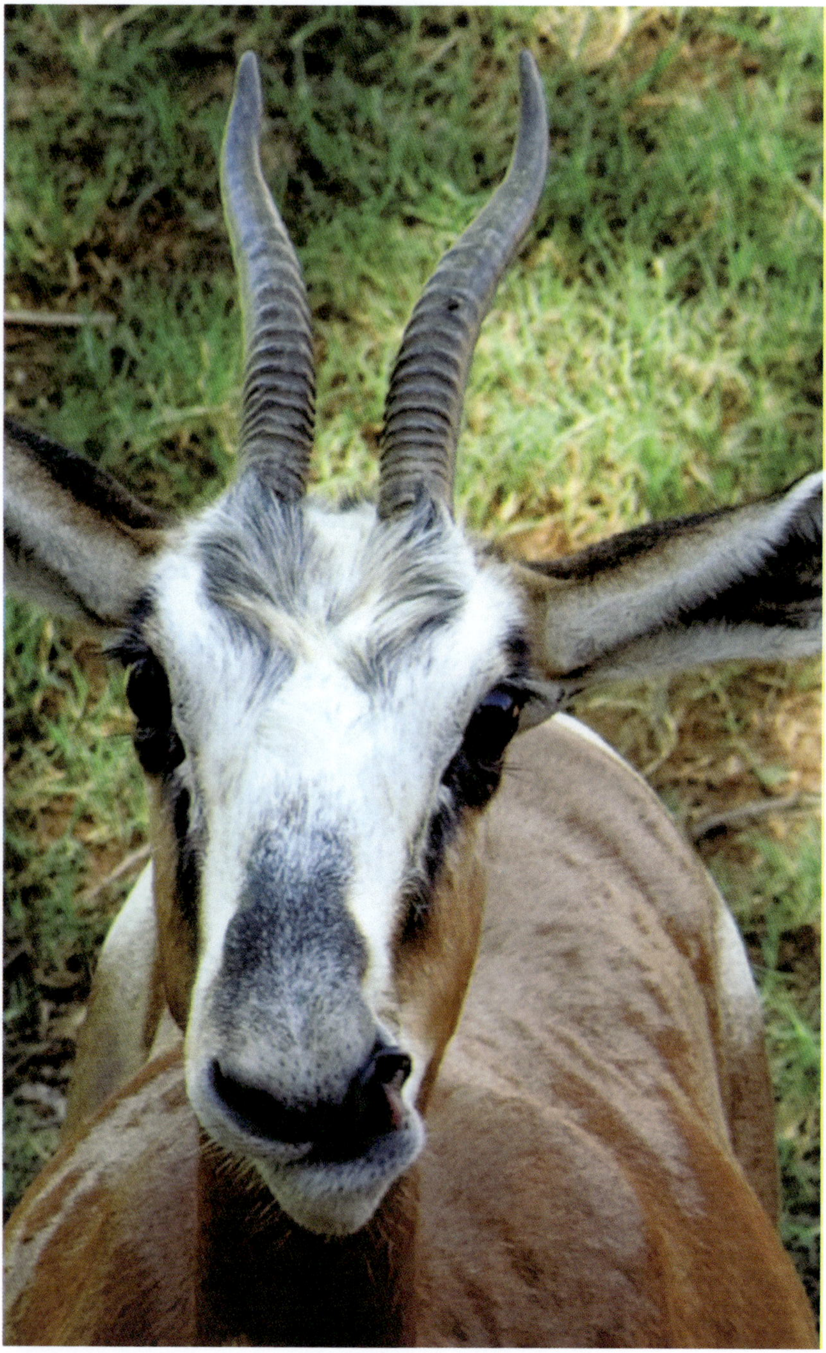

COLOR ME

COLOR ME

COLOR ME

COLOR ME

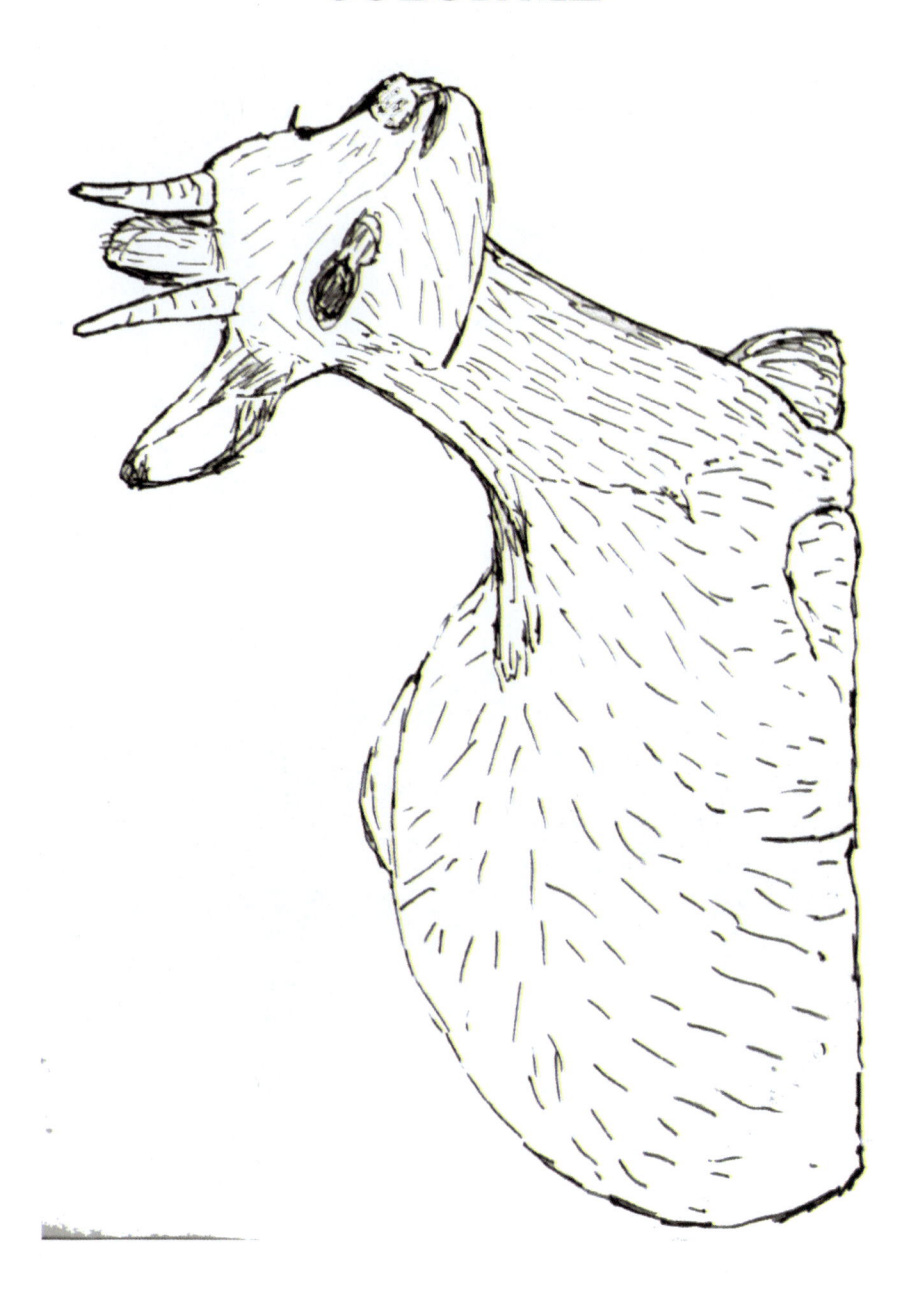

COLOR ME

COLOR ME

COLOR ME

COLOR ME

COLOR ME

COLOR ME

Please leave me a review here:

LisaStrattin.com/Review-Vol-126

For more Kindle Downloads Visit Lisa Strattin Author Page on Amazon Author Central

amazon.com/author/lisastrattin

To see upcoming titles, visit my website at LisaStrattin.com– most books available on Kindle!

LisaStrattin.com

FREE BOOK

FOR ALL SUBSCRIBERS – SIGN UP NOW

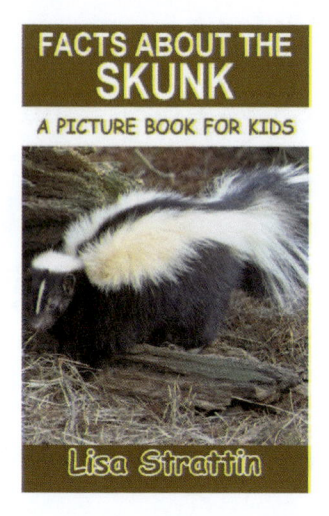

LisaStrattin.com/Subscribe-Here

LisaStrattin.com/Facebook

LisaStrattin.com/Youtube

Printed in Great Britain
by Amazon